GRAMMAR Book

Michael Temple

CONTENTS

1. Words Often Confused

(See also common faults, sub-section 10, p. 31)

accept
to receive
except
to omit, exclude; not including

accessary
one who aids (e.g. in a crime)
accessory
an attachment or extra
(e.g. to a dress or car)

adapt
to adjust
adopt
to accept and approve, take as one's own

affect (verb)
to influence or produce an effect on
effect (noun or verb)
a result; to bring about or accomplish

aggravate
to make worse
irritate
to annoy, exasperate

alibi
fact or claim that one was elsewhere
excuse
apology offered

allowed
permitted
aloud
audibly, loudly

allusion (to)
casual or indirect reference
illusion
false impression or image; magician's trick
delusion
deception, mistaken belief

already
by this time
all ready
all persons (things) are ready

alternate
by turns
alternative
either of two possible courses

altogether
completely
all together
all in one place

always
ever, constantly
all ways
all directions or methods

amiable
likeable
amicable
friendly

amount
How much? (weight or money)
number
How many? (individual items)

astrology
foretelling the future by the stars
astronomy
science of the planets and stars

bail
security for a court appearance; on cricket stumps
bale
bundle; to jump out of a plane (as verbs, both mean to scoop out water)

bare
naked; to uncover
bear
to carry; an animal

beside
at the side of
besides
in addition to

board
plank, table; to receive meals; to go on board
bored
weary with tediousness; made a hole

boarder
lodger (with meals)
border
edge, limit

born
come into the world by birth
borne
carried, endured

brake
to put the brakes on (e.g. a car)
break
to shatter; interval

breath (verb)
air drawn into lungs
breathe (noun)
to draw air into lungs

Britain
the country
Briton
the inhabitant

broach (verb)
to open (e.g. a barrel or a subject for discussion)
brooch (noun)
an ornament

cannon
a gun
canon
a churchman; church law

canvas
coarse cloth for a tent, etc.
canvass
to solicit votes, orders, etc.

ceremonial (adj. or noun)
of a ritual or ceremony, formal
ceremonious
too much concerned with formalities, showy

check
stop; test for correctness; pattern of squares
cheque
bank draft or bill

choose
(present tense)
chose
(past tense of to choose)

civic
of a city
civil
polite; not military (e.g. "Civil Service")

climactic
of a climax
climatic
of climate

coarse
rough, harsh, crude
course
for racing, golf; the division of a meal; a series; "of course"

compare
to point out similarities
contrast
to point out differences

complement
that which makes up or completes
compliment
praise

contemporary
existing at the same time as
modern
up-to-date

contemptible
vile, mean
contemptuous
showing or feeling scorn

continual
frequent, repeated
(e.g. dripping tap)
continuous
connected, unbroken
(e.g. stream of water)

council
an assembly
counsel
advice; legal adviser; to advise

credible
believable
creditable
deserving praise

credulous
inclined to believe; gullible
currant
small berry
current
now running, in general use; flow of water, electricity, air

decease
death
disease
illness

defective
faulty
deficient
lacking

dependant (noun)
one who depends on another
dependent (adj.)
depending on

definite
fixed, certain, clear
definitive
final, complete, thorough

deprecate
to express disapproval of
depreciate
to go down in value, rate less highly

derisive
showing contempt
derisory
deserving contempt

desert
barren place; that which is deserved; to abandon
dessert
sweet course in a meal

detract (from)
to lessen; take away from
distract
to divert (attention)

disburse
to pay out money
disperse
to scatter, spread (or vanish)

discover
to find something which was always there
invent
to create or devise something new

disinterested
neutral, unbiased
uninterested
lacking interest, not interested

draft
rough copy or plan; draw up a bill, money order; selection for army
draught
all other senses: e.g. air current; beer on…; ship's displacement; game of draughts

drawers
chest of…
draws
verb to draw; drawn games; attractions

dual
double, composed of two
duel
fight between two people

economic
of a country's finances; profitable
economical
being careful, thrifty

effective
having an effect; coming into operation
effectual
answering its purpose
efficacious
sure to produce the desired effect
efficient
competent; working productively

elicit (verb)
to draw out
illicit
not legal

eligible
fit to be chosen
illegible
indecipherable

emigrant
one who leaves the country
immigrant
one who enters the country

eminent
prominent, distinguished
imminent
threatening, near at hand

ensure
to make sure
insure
to take out an insurance policy

envelop (verb)
to surround or cover
envelope (noun)
for a letter

especially
notably, particularly
specially
for a special occasion or purpose

exceptionable
objectionable
exceptional
unusual

fact
a truth, actual happening
factor
a contributory element, cause

faint
to swoon; dim, indistinct, weak
feint
sham attack, or blow; pretence (both mean pale in phrase "faint / feint lines")

fatal
resulting in death
fateful
deciding one's fate

flaunt
show off
flout
to express contempt for (e.g. authority), defy

flowed
past participle of to flow (water)
flown
past participle of to fly (birds)

foregoing
preceding, gone before
forgoing
giving up, abstaining from

formally
in a formal manner
formerly
previously

fortuitous
happening by chance
fortunate
having or bringing good luck

genteel
affectedly elegant
gentle
not rough

hanged
executed ("hanged by the neck")
hung
other uses of the verb to hang

hear
to perceive sound, listen to
here
at this place

hoard
store
horde
crowd

human
of man as opposed to animal or god
humane
compassionate, kind

idle
lazy
idol
object of worship

imaginary
of a thing that exists only in the imagination
imaginative
having a high degree of imagination

imperial
of an empire or emperor
imperious
proud, domineering

imply
to hint (speaker implies)
infer
to draw a conclusion (hearer infers)

impracticable
that cannot be put into effect
unpractical
not having practical skill; not suited to actual conditions

industrial
of industry
industrious
hard-working

ingenious
skilful in inventing
ingenuous
artless, innocent

intellectual
of the mind, having superior powers of reasoning; a person who is concerned with things of the mind (as opposed to feelings)
intelligent
clever
intelligible
clear, understandable

into
entering, inside (e.g. He went into the house.)
in to
(separate senses) (e.g. She came in to tell us the news.)

it's
it is (or it has)
its
belonging to it

judicial
connected with a judge or law court
judicious
having sound judgement

larva
caterpillar, etc.
lava
from a volcano

lead
metal; (present tense of to lead)
led
(past tense of to lead)

leant
(past tense of to lean)
lent
(past tense of to lend)

less
smaller in amount
fewer
smaller in number

lightening
making less heavy or less dark
lightning
a flash of

loath/loth
reluctant, unwilling
loathe
to dislike greatly

loose
to unfasten; not tight
lose
to fail to win; fail to keep

luxuriant
growing profusely
luxurious
very comfortable; self-indulgent

marshal (noun or verb)
officer; to arrange in due order
martial (adj.)
of war or the army (court-martialled)

masterful
imperious, domineering
masterly
expert, skilful

maybe
perhaps
may be
e.g. it may be…

meter
gas, electric, parking (measuring machine)
metre
measure of distance; verse rhythm

momentary
short-lived
momentous
important

moral
right, virtuous; lesson from a story
morale
mental state of confidence

negligent
careless
negligible
small or unimportant

new
opposite of old
knew
past tense of to know

notable
worth noting
noticeable
easy to see, prominent

observance
obeying, paying heed to (a rule or custom)
observation
noting, looking at

official
connected with an office; authorised
officious
meddlesome

oral
spoken (of the mouth)
aural
pertaining to the ear
verbal
in words (spoken or written)

partake of
to take part or share (food or rest)
participate
to take part in

peace
opposite of war; quiet
piece
a portion or part

persecute
to oppress, harass
prosecute
to take legal proceedings against

personal
individual, private
personnel
employees or staff

plain
flat country; clear; undecorated; unattractive
plane
level surface; to shave level; tool; tree; aeroplane

pray
to worship, beg
prey
hunted animal; plunder

precede
to go before in arrangement or rank
proceed
to go along, continue

precipitate
hasty, rash
precipitous
steep

prescribe
to order, lay down as a rule
proscribe
to condemn, prohibit

principal
chief, most important
principle (noun)
truth, law, idea; code of conduct

quiet
silent
quite
fairly, very, completely

rain
water from the clouds
reign
a king's
reins
a horse's

raise(d)
to lift, make grow, increase
raze/rase
to demolish, level to the ground
rise (rose)
to get up or go up

recourse
"to have recourse to" (to resort to)
resource
source of supply; device; ingenuity

re-cover
to cover again
recover
to regain health, regain possession of

re-form
to form again
reform
to correct, improve

re-sign
to sign again
resign
to give up (e.g. a job or office)

respectable
worthy of respect
respectful
showing respect
respective
relating to each in order

review
survey, inspection
revue
a stage production
right
opposite of left or wrong; just claim or due

rite
ceremony (religious)
write
with a pen, etc.

scarce
of ordinary things temporarily not plentiful
rare
of things infrequent at all times

seasonable
suitable to the occasion or season
seasonal
occurring at a particular season

sensible
showing good sense
sensitive
capable of feeling deeply; responsive to slight changes

sensual
indulging the senses
sensuous
relating to the senses

sew
i.e. with a needle
sow
i.e. with seeds

shear
to shave, cut
sheer
steep; absolute; transparent; to swerve

sight
thing seen; faculty of vision
site
location, position, plot

sociable
enjoying company
social
pertaining to society

solidarity
show of support for, holding the same interest as
solidity
state of being firm, stable or solid

stalactite
comes down from "ceiling" of a cave
stalagmite
grows up from the ground

stationary
not moving
stationery
writing materials

stimulant
alcohol, drug
stimulus
incentive

superficial
on the surface, shallow
superfluous
too many, more than is needed

taught
past tense of to teach
taut
tight, tense

temporal
earthly (as opposed to spiritual or eternal)
temporary
not permanent

their
belonging to them
there
in that place; there is
they're
they are

threw
past tense of to throw
through
from one end or side to the other; by means of
thorough
complete, in detail; very careful

to
always used except for:
too
also or in an excessive degree ("too hot")
two
number

translucent
allowing light through but not transparent
transparent
that can be seen through

urban
of a town
urbane
well-bred, suave, civilised

waist
part of body
waste (noun)
rubbish, barren land
waive
to set aside, forgo (a claim, right, rule)
wave
shake or move to and fro; curve(s) of water, hair, sound, heat, etc.

weather
sunshine, wind, rain, etc.
whether
if

were
past tense of to be
we're
we are
where
in what place?

who's
who is (or has)
whose
belonging to whom

your
belonging to you
you're
you are

2. Punctuation

(See also useful terms, p. 22)

1 The full stop

(a) marks the end of a sentence (except for questions and exclamations). A sentence is a complete unit of sense which can stand on its own. (It may consist of only one word as in greetings like "Hello.", commands like "Stop." (where the 'subject' – you – is understood), and replies like "No.").

To test whether a group of words is a sentence, you should read it out to yourself; if it conveys a complete meaning, then you can probably put a full stop at the end. However, you must check the next 'sentence' in the same way.

(b) indicates an abbreviation. (It is only essential where the shortened form does *not* contain the last letter of the word.)
e.g. Co. etc. i.e. a.m. – *but* Mr Dr

(Full stops are often omitted in abbreviations formed from initial capitals: e.g. BBC, TUC, MP (plural MPs).)

A series of three dots marks a breaking off. It is also useful when you are referring to a long extract and wish to give the first and last few words only. (The omitted section is covered by the three dots.)

2 Capital letters are used

(a) at the beginning of every sentence

(b) at the beginning of a passage of direct speech (see 6 below).

(c) for proper nouns (i.e. names of *particular* persons, places, things), and for months of the year and days of the week:
e.g. Jane, Everest, Liverpool, July, Monday

(d) for adjectives derived from proper nouns (especially places and people):
e.g. English, French, Victorian, Elizabethan (except for common compounds like brussels sprouts and venetian blinds, where the adjective has lost its original emphasis).

(e) for the first and all main words in *any kind of title*:
books, plays, poems (e.g. 'Far from the Madding Crowd')
films, T.V. programmes (e.g. 'Panorama')
newspapers and magazines (e.g. 'The Times')
names of ships, houses, inns
a person's title (e.g. Archbishop of York)
the titles of institutions and businesses (e.g. Women's Institute)
abbreviations of such titles (e.g. M.P.)

(f) at the beginning of each line of verse (except in some modern poetry.)

(g) for the pronoun 'I'.

(h) when a noun is personified or considered as a grand abstract idea:
e.g 'The Child is Father of the Man.'

(i) for 'He', 'His', when referring to God.

3 The question mark

This is used for all direct questions:
e.g. What are you doing?
You will come, won't you?

but *not* for reported questions:
e.g I wonder what he is doing.
Ask him who did it.

(Don't forget the question mark at the end of a long question.)

4 The exclamation mark

This expresses some kind of astonishment or a sharp outburst or comment:
e.g. Fire! Fire!

It can also add a tone of humour or sarcasm:
e.g. You're a fine one to talk!

(Don't over-use it and don't use more than one at a time.)

5 Commas

The following rules cover the main uses. (You will find that there are many other optional uses which lend emphasis or give a finer point of meaning.)

Commas are used:

(a) to separate words, phrases or clauses in a list:

(i) a series of nouns
e.g. His room was littered with books, pens, papers and maps.

(ii) a series of adjectives:
e.g. He was a quiet, gentle, unassuming man.

When one adjective describes the other or when the last adjective is closely linked with its noun, there should be no comma:
e.g. the deep blue sky; a new Cambridge college

(Contrast: a thin, white hand)

(iii) a series of adverbs:
e.g. Try to work quickly, confidently and efficiently.

(iv) a series of phrases:
e.g. We spent an enjoyable day visiting the zoo, rowing on the lake, and picnicking in the park.

(v) a series of verbs or clauses:
e.g. He took a long run-up, slipped on the wet grass, and landed short of the sand-pit.

(It is better with larger groupings to put a comma before the 'and'.)

The comma is also used between two long main clauses joined by 'and' or 'but', especially when the subjects of the clauses are different.

(b) before and after a phrase or clause in apposition (i.e. when placing a group of words after a noun to give a fuller explanation or description of it):
e.g. Jean, *Bill's elder sister*, brought home a new hat, *a pink one with feathers*.

(c) to separate 'sentence adverbs' – these show the link between the whole sentence and the preceding one(s):
e.g. however, on the other hand, moreover
They tried hard. The conditions, *however*, were against them.

(d) to mark off the person(s) addressed or called to (whether by name or other description):
e.g. Look out, *Fred!* Now, *you fool*, you've missed it!

(e) to bracket off insertions or afterthoughts. (Dashes or brackets may also be used for this.) Use commas on either side of the parenthesis:
e.g. Sunday, *as everyone knows*, is a day of rest.

(f) to mark off interjections – words like 'yes', 'no', 'please':
e.g. *Well, er, no*, I don't think I will, *thank you*.

(g) before 'tagging on' clauses like 'don't you?' or 'isn't it?'
e.g. They played well, *didn't they*?

(h) to mark off a participial phrase:
e.g. *Seeing the lion*, Caesar screamed.

(i) to mark off adverbial clauses, especially when they start the sentence, except when they are very short. (Adverbial clauses are introduced by words like 'although', 'if', 'because'.)
e.g. *Although you may not realise it*, you need two commas in this sentence, *because it contains two adverbial clauses*.

(j) to mark off an adjective clause which merely comments but does not limit or define:
e.g. The boys, *who were fooling*, were punished.

(*Without* commas this would mean that *only* the boys who were fooling were punished; *with* commas it means that *all* the boys were fooling and were punished. The commas act like brackets.)

N.B. Don't put a comma between the subject and its verb:

WRONG: What he wrote, was illegible.
RIGHT: What he wrote was illegible.

6 Punctuating conversation/direct speech

(a) Start a new paragraph *every* time the speaker changes.

(b) The words spoken and the accompanying punctuation are enclosed in inverted commas (double or single). (N.B. The punctuation comes *inside* the inverted commas.)

(c) Even though the words spoken would form a sentence on their own, they are followed by a comma (not a full stop) when the verb of saying and its subject come *afterwards*:
e.g. "We are going away," they said.
but "Where are you going?" he asked.

(d) When the subject and verb of saying start the sentence, they are followed by a comma, and the first word spoken has a capital letter:
e.g. They said, "We are going away."

(e) When the 'spoken sentence' is interrupted to insert the verb of saying and its subject, one comma is needed when breaking off the speech and another immediately before continuing it. The next word within the inverted commas has a small letter, because it is continuing the spoken sentence:
e.g. "I am not," he stressed, "particularly happy about this."

Consider the following two sentences:
"I am going," he said. "Do not try to stop me."

7 Inverted commas are also used

(a) when quoting someone's words or from a book:
e.g. A famous speech from 'Hamlet' begins "To be or not to be".

(The full stop comes after the inverted commas. Contrast 6(b) above. No comma after 'begins'. Contrast 6(d) above.)

Take care, when quoting from a book/play/poem, that your own sentence leads naturally into the quotation.

(b) for titles of books, plays, T.V. programmes, films, newspapers, house-names, names of ships, inns etc.:
e.g. Two of the most famous Elizabethan theatres were 'The Globe' and 'The Fortune'.
(Book or play titles may instead be underlined in writing or italicised in print.)

(c) when using foreign words, jargon, specialist words or slang; or to show that a word is used sarcastically. (In print these might be italicised.)

N.B. Use *single* inverted commas within direct speech:
e.g. "Did you enjoy 'Pygmalion'?" he asked.

But if you use single inverted commas for speech – see sub-section 6(b) – then use double inverted commas within.
e.g. However, on the other hand, moreover
They tried hard. The conditions, *however*, were against them

8 The apostrophe is used

(a) to denote *possession* with nouns. The singular noun takes an apostrophe followed by an 's'. Plurals ending in an 's' add an apostrophe after the final 's':
e.g. a lady's hat, the ladies' hats (i.e. the hats of the ladies)
a week's holiday, six weeks' holiday
an ass's burden, Dickens's novels, Charles's sister
Jones's cap, the Joneses' house (i.e. the house of the Joneses)

Be careful with unusual plurals (like men, children, mice) which are treated as if they were singular:
e.g. men's coats, women's rights, children's toys
(*never* write mens' or childrens')

For proper nouns ending in a sounded 'e' and an 's' or in 's' vowel's' (e.g. Euripides, Moses) add the apostrophe after the 's':
e.g. Ulysses' adventures, Archimedes' principle, Jesus' mother

(Note also – for goodness' sake.)

In units involving two or more nouns or in a compound noun or phrase, put the apostrophe on the last word only:
e.g. William and Mary's reign, my father-in-law's house, the Leader of the Opposition's speech

This does not apply if there is no joint possession:
e.g. my brother's and my sister's birthdays

N.B. The apostrophe is *not* used in these words: yours, hers, ours, theirs or its (when it means belonging to it). (Would you write *hi's* for his?) It is, however, used in *one's* (belonging to one and one is/one has).

(b) to indicate a *contraction*. The apostrophe is placed where the letter(s) has (have) been omitted:
e.g. didn't, can't, they're (they are), you're, we're, I'd, I'll, it's (meaning it is or it has), fo'c's'le
(But note: shan't, won't.)

(c) for the plural form of certain *letters* and *figures*, although this apostrophe is now often omitted:
e.g. the three R's, P's and Q's, in the 60's, if's and but's

Do not put an apostrophe in ordinary noun plurals.

9 Dashes and brackets

Two dashes are used when breaking off a sentence to insert an afterthought or an explanatory comment or short list:
e.g. In August last year – I was with my family at the time – I had a serious accident.
Nothing – food, plates, cutlery, pans – could be left unattended.

A single dash may be used

(a) when breaking off a sentence for an abrupt change of thought or when 'tagging on' another construction:
e.g. The following day we had better luck – but that is another story.

(b) to emphasise a repeated word:
e.g. The new regime imposed rigid laws – laws which the police found difficult to operate.

(c) when bringing together a number of items:
e.g. Toothbrush, tin-opener, matches, scourer – these are often forgotten by inexperienced campers.

(d) with a colon to introduce a long quotation or list, although this usage is now dying out (this is called a pointer :–)

(e) to signify missing letters:
e.g. D– – – it!

Brackets (always two) are, like dashes, used for 'asides' and for enclosing additional information:
e.g. Citrus fruits (oranges, lemons, limes) are rich in vitamin C.

(Brackets like dashes, often carry the meaning of 'that is' (i.e.) or 'namely'.)

(If there is a bracketed *phrase* at the end of a sentence, the full stop follows the bracket; if the brackets enclose a *sentence*, the full stop comes inside.)

10 The hyphen is used

(a) when attaching a prefix (e.g. multi-storey, anti-aircraft, by-product) and especially when confusion might result as with re-sign and re-form. (It also splits vowel sounds as in re-elected.)

(b) when forming a compound word from two or more other words:
e.g. son-in-law, a half-eaten biscuit, a couldn't-care-less attitude, red-hot, swimming-bath, smoking-jacket

Distinguish 'fifty-odd people' from 'fifty odd people'.

(The hyphen is also used when splitting a word between syllables at the end of a line.)

11 The semicolon is, or may be, used

(a) to separate clauses which could stand as sentences but which are *closely related*, especially

(i) when the second clause *expands* or explains the first:
e.g. Neither of us spoke; we merely waited in silence to see what would happen.

(ii) when the clauses describe a *sequence* of actions or *different aspects* of the *same* topic:
e.g. There was a sharp, bracing air; the ground was dry; the sea was crisp and clear.

(iii) before 'sentences' beginning with 'even so', 'so', 'therefore', 'for instance', 'nevertheless', 'then' etc.:
e.g. He took great care; even so, he made a few errors.

(iv) to suggest a contrast:
e.g. I like swimming; my sister hates it.

(In all the above examples full stops could have been used but would have been too abrupt.)

Note that the clause or 'sentence' after the semicolon always begins with a small letter.

(b) to mark off a series of phrases (or clauses) which themselves contain commas. (Compare the use of square and round brackets in mathematics.)
e.g. You will need the following: some scrap paper; a pen, preferably blue or black; some envelopes; and some good, white, unlined writing-paper.

12 The colon is used

(a) to introduce a list (e.g. as in 11(b) above), long quotation or speech:

e.g. Speaking at Caesar's funeral, Antony addresses the crowd: "Friends, Romans, countrymen…"

It may also be used

(b) before a clause which explains (often by illustration) the previous statement. The colon has the force of the word 'namely' or 'that is':

e.g. One thing is certain: we shall not surrender. (Here a dash could have been used.)

(c) to express a *strong* contrast:

e.g. God creates: man destroys.

(d) to introduce a climax or concluding clause:

e.g. After pondering the choices before him, he came to a decision: he joined the army.

(e) to make a pointed connection:

e.g. Jeremy became a director in just three months: his father was the chief shareholder.

3. Formal Letters

Letter-writing is a branch of good manners. You will often be judged on the letters you write – to prospective employers, for instance.

The following notes apply to formal or official letters.

1 Paper

It is important to use *good*, preferably *white, unlined* paper (and to choose a size to match the length of your letter). It is always best to rough out your letter first – it can serve as your reference copy – as this will help you avoid mistakes, save expensive notepaper and give you an idea of the spacing and layout of the letter, enabling you to avoid crossings-out or signing off just over the page. Check your expression, punctuation and spelling. If you do make a mistake which requires crossing out, scrap the letter and rewrite the whole.

2 Addressing envelopes

Envelopes should match the paper.

(a) Layout

J. Blank, Esq.,	The Personnel Manager,
100 Blank Street,	John Murray (Publishers) Ltd,
BLANKTON,	50 Albermarle Street,
Blankshire,	LONDON,
PO2 8QT	W1X 4BD

Write a legible address with a postcode. (Punctuation at the ends of lines is not essential. You may 'stagger' each line of the address.)

Note:

(i) Name/title of person and/or of firm.
(ii) Number (or name) of house and road name.
(iii) Name of village or local district where applicable.
(iv) Post town in CAPITALS.
(v) County where applicable. Write it in full (or use the official abbreviation, e.g. Oxon.)
(vi) Postcode in capitals, preferably on a separate line.
(vii) Leave space at the top for the postmark.

(b) Warnings

(i) Remember that you are writing to a particular person. Use his name or his office/title:
e.g. The Registrar, The Principal, The Personnel Officer

(ii) Write *either* J. Blank, Esq.
or Mr J. Blank
never Mr J. Blank, Esq.
(Initials denoting qualifications, e.g. M.Sc., should follow the Esq.)

(iii) Beneath this, your signature (*legibly*) written.

3 The letter

(a) Layout

Leave a margin space of at least 2.5 centimetres down the left-hand side and at top and bottom, and 1.5 centimetres down the right-hand side.

(Your address – like this or staggered)

5 Blank Street,
Blankton,
Blanksire.

(Addressee) (Date in full) 27 February 1997

The Registrar,
Leeds University,
Leeds.

Dear Sir,

....

....

Yours faithfully,

(Signature)

(or centred for written letters)

(The name and address of the addressee may instead be put in the bottom left corner, and, as on envelopes, punctuation at the ends of lines in addresses may be omitted. If you need to quote a reference number, put it in the top left corner.)

Notes on layout:

(i) Date in full, *not* 29.2.97 or Feb. 29th, etc., (but abbreviations for postcards).

(ii) 'Yours faithfully,' on the left-hand side below the message. (N.B. comma following.)

(iii) Beneath this, your signature *legibly* written.

(b) Mode of address and signing off

If you do not know the addressee, use 'Dear Sir,' and sign off 'Yours faithfully,'. If you know him, or have previously written to him, use 'Dear Mr Blank,' and sign off 'Yours sincerely,'. (No capital for 'sincerely' or 'faithfully'.)

(c) General

In general, aim at clarity, conciseness and dignity of expression. Be polite and direct. Avoid verbosity and business jargon (e.g. 'We are in receipt of your highly esteemed favour of the 16th ult.'), as well as colloquialisms, slang and contractions.

If you are replying to a letter, you should normally first thank the sender thus: 'Thank you for your letter of 16 January.'

Start a new paragraph for your message. (It is common now, particularly in business letters, not to indent the first line of a paragraph. Instead, paragraphs are separated by spaces between them. This is also often done in books that consist of notes rather than continuous text – as this book does.)

When making requests, you will find the following a useful construction: 'I should be grateful if you would . . .'

When applying for a job, you could use a heading note before or after the 'Dear Sir,': e.g. Ref.: (Advertisement) in 'The Daily Globe', 12.10.97 (the date may be abbreviated in such cases).

(If you are writing to Lords, Queens or Bishops, you should consult a book of etiquette!)

In letters of a more friendly nature (not 'chatty' letters to the family) you may be more expansive and personal in style, but must judge the *tone* tactfully and adapt sensibly to the demands of the occasion. Think of the impression your letter gives and imagine yourself in the place of the recipient. Have you assumed the right manner? Have you given the information required in a clear, orderly fashion? Have you made your requests clearly? As with all forms of writing, some forethought and planning are needed. (Note: A friendly letter should not contain the address of the person you are writing to and should end with 'Yours sincerely,' , 'With best wishes,' or something similar – keep your 'fun' endings for your close friends and relations.)

4. Useful Terms

GRAMMATICAL

Language employs the following units: **(i)** single words, **(ii)** phrases, **(iii)** clauses, **(iv)** sentences, **(v)** paragraphs.

1 Parts of speech (i.e. the different jobs done by words)

(a) A **noun** names a person, thing or quality:
e.g. boy, John, brick, beauty, decision.

(b) A **pronoun** stands in place of a noun (to avoid repeating it):
e.g. he, him, me, it, they, them, you, anyone, who, whom.

(c) A **verb** expresses an action (or state of being):
e.g. he *ran*, he *is*… , I *will* go.
(It has several tenses which show when the action takes place.)

(d) An **adjective** describes a noun (or pronoun). It can either stand in front of a noun or refer back to it:
e.g. a *black* cat; *my own* work; the *quick brown* fox; the street is *long*.

(e) An **adverb** usually 'modifies' a verb, telling how, where, when or why an action is done. (It can also modify an adjective or another adverb.) Except for very common adverbs, it usually ends in '-ly':
e.g. He ran *quickly*; (*very* good; *extremely* well)

(f) A **conjunction** joins, or shows the relationship between, words, phrases or clauses (see 5(b) below):
e.g. fish *and* chips; poor *but* honest; for better *or* for worse; he played well, *although* he was injured.

(g) A **preposition** introduces a phrase and is followed by a noun or pronoun (which it 'governs'):
e.g. Put it *on* the table; *by* air; *up* the pole; *over* the hills; *between* you and me.

(h) An **interjection** is an exclamatory word (or phrase). It can be taken out of the sentence without destroying the sense:
e.g. *Well, er, no, oh dear, ugh!*

Nouns and pronouns as 'subject', 'direct object' and 'complement'

The **subject** is the person or thing doing the action (or being something):
e.g. Jack built *the house*. *He* hit me. *She* was a nurse.

The **direct object** is the person or thing affected by the action.

(It answers the question 'Whom?' or 'What?')
e.g. Jack built *the house* (The object – 'house' – is what he built.)
He hit *me*.

The **complement** completes the sense of verbs like 'to be', 'to become', and 'to seem':
e.g. He is *an actor.*

The **personal pronouns** in the subject (nominative) case are as follows (the object – accusative – pronouns are given only where they differ):

	Singular (i.e. one)	**Plural** (i.e. more than one)
1st person	I (me)	we (us)
2nd person	you	you
3rd person	he/she/it (him/her)	they (them)

2 Phrases

A phrase is a group of words (two or more) which acts as a noun, adjective or adverb:
e.g. To *write well* requires practice. (The italicised phrase acts as a noun, 'subject' of the verb 'requires'.)
The boy *wearing the blue vest* came second. (Adjective phrase describing the noun 'boy'.)
Put it *on the table*. (Adverb phrase, telling where the action is to be done.)

3 Simple sentences

A simple sentence contains one finite verb, i.e. a verb used with its subject. The subject, in person and number, determines the form of the verb:
e.g. John *sings* well.
(A finite verb may consist of several verbs which make up its tense: e.g. John *should have been playing*, but he was ill.)

4 Clauses

A clause is a group of words containing a finite verb. There are two basic types:

(a) Main clause – the 'backbone' of the sentence. It often makes a simple sentence on its own (but see noun clauses below).

(b) Subordinate clause – this, like a phrase, acts as an adjective, adverb or noun, and depends upon the main clause.

5 Types of subordinate clause

(a) Adjective clause

e.g. The man *who called yesterday* must have been a salesman. (The italicised words describe 'the man'.)
I found the book (*that*) *I had been searching for.* (Describes 'book'.)
He was absent on the day *when it happened* (Describes 'day'.)

(b) Adverb clause

There are various kinds:

(i) Time:
e.g. The crowd cheered *when the Queen appeared.* (When?)

(ii) Place:
e.g. He hid the gold *where no one would find it.* (Where?)

(iii) Reason:
e.g. He won *because he had more stamina.* (Why?)

(iv) Purpose:
e.g. He worked hard *so that he would pass his exam.* (With what intention?)

(v) Result:
e.g. They played so well *that they won the cup.* (With what result?)

(vi) Condition:
e.g. You will succeed *if you try hard.* (On what condition?)

(vii) Concession:
e.g. *Although they played well,* they still lost. (In spite of what?)

(viii) Manner:
e.g. They did *as they pleased.* (How?)

(ix) Degree (or **comparison**):
e.g. He sings better *than I do.* (To what extent? Compared with what?)

(c) The **noun clause** may

(i) be the **subject** of the main verb:
e.g. *Why he did it* remains a mystery.

(ii) be the **direct object** of the main verb:
e.g. I do not know *whether he will come.*

(iii) be the **complement** of a verb of being:
e.g. This is *how we do it.*

(iv) be **in apposition** to a previous noun or pronoun (i.e. when enlarging upon or re-stating it):
e.g. The idea *that he could be guilty* never crossed our minds.
It never crossed our minds *that he was guilty*.

(v) follow a **preposition**:
e.g. The point of *what he said* eludes me.
He gave an account of *when it happened*.

In all of the above examples in **(a), (b)** and **(c)**, the words not italicised form the main clause.

A sentence containing a main clause and one or more subordinate clauses is called a **complex** sentence. A sentence containing two or more main clauses (joined by 'and', 'but', 'or') is called a **compound** sentence; it may also contain subordinate clauses.

6 Paragraphs

A paragraph is a set of sentences (sometimes just one) developing *one* topic. (Make sure that you indent the first line clearly, but see Section 3, sub-section 3(c) for letters.)

7 Non-finite verb-forms

These are *incomplete* forms.

(a) The **infinitive**
e.g. *to walk, to be considered, to have seen*

(b) **Participles.** The present participle ends in '-ing'; the past in '-ed' (usually).

A participle may

(i) act as an adjective
e.g. a talking doll

(ii) introduce to an adjective phrase:
e.g. Talking very loudly, they got on the train.

(iii) help form a finite verb with other verb-parts:
e.g. I had been talking to him.

Note: the '-ing' ending may denote a gerund (a *noun*):
e.g. Talking is forbidden.

8 Active and passive

When the subject is performing the action, the verb is said to be in the 'active voice':
e.g. Jack *built* the house.

When the subject is suffering the action, the verb is said to be in the 'passive voice':
e.g. The house *was built* by Jack.

9 Transitive and intransitive verbs

A **transitive** verb takes an object:
e.g. He woke *his brother*. She boiled *an egg*. (Objects italicised.)
An **intransitive** verb does not:
e.g. He awoke. The water boiled.

10 Indirect objects

The indirect object is the person (or thing) *to* or *for* whom the action is done:
e.g. Pass the ball to *him*. He gave *me* a book. ('me' means 'to me'.)

11 Prefixes

A prefix is a small group of letters (often from Latin or Greek) put at the beginning of a word to alter its meaning:
e.g. *mis*fire; *anti*-aircraft; *extra*ordinary

12 Suffixes

A suffix is a group of letters attached to the end of a word to change its function or its meaning:
e.g. The suffix '-ly' turns an adjective into an adverb:
'careful' (adjective) becomes 'carefully' (adverb).
e.g. 'wright' (meaning 'workman') as in 'wheelwright' and 'playwright'.

LITERARY

(a) Imagery creates vivid pictures or sensations in the mind by likening one thing to another; it includes metaphors and similes. (A poem may be an extended image or set of images.)

(b) A **simile** brings out a point (or points) of likeness between two different things. It is usually introduced by the word 'like' or 'as':
e.g. Her skin was *as white as snow*.
His hand was trembling *like a leaf*.

(c) A **metaphor** is a condensed simile (without the word 'like' or 'as'). One thing is said to be the other thing with which it is compared.
e.g. The train *snaked* its way up the valley.
That boy is an *ass*.

(d) Personification is treating an abstract quality (like justice or Honour) as if it were human:
e.g. Hope had grown grey hairs.

It is also commonly used to endow non-human things with human feelings:
e.g. The kettle sang merrily.

('Pathetic fallacy' is ascribing human feelings to nature:
e.g. the angry winds, the kind old sun.)

(e) A **symbol** is an object (or set of objects) standing for some idea:
e.g. The *cross* is the symbol of Christianity.

(f) An **allegory** is a story which carries another and deeper meaning; the story stands for or suggests something else:
e.g. 'The Ancient Mariner' is an allegory about guilt.
'Animal Farm' is a political allegory.
(An allegory is a longer version of a parable.)

(g) A **pun** is a play on words, either on two meanings of the same word, or on words sounding alike:
e.g. Drilling holes is *boring*
Was King Kong the original urban *guerrilla*?

(h) **Hyperbole** is exaggeration for effect:
e.g. Dinner took *ages*.

(i) A **paradox** is a saying which seems to contradict itself; its apparent nonsense, however, emphasises a truth:
e.g. More haste, less speed.

(j) A **euphemism** is a mild or indirect way of describing an unpleasant or embarrassing thing:
e.g. He passed away; a water-closet.

(k) **Irony**

(i) **Verbal** – when you mean the opposite of what the words state:
e.g. You're a nice one!
Antony in 'Julius Caesar' calls Caesar's assassins 'honourable men' but means the opposite.

(ii) **Dramatic** – when the audience knows something that one or all of the characters on the stage don't know.

(l) **Onomatopoeia** is using words which, through their own *sound*, imitate or suggest the sound of what they describe:
e.g. miaow, buzz; the blare of trumpets; the murmuring of innumerable bees

(m) **Alliteration** is the repeating of sounds (usually consonants at the beginnings of words) to echo the sense or sound of the thing described:
e.g. the stuttering rifle's rapid rattle …
The fair breeze blew, the white foam flew,
The furrow followed free; …
(Assonance is repeating vowel sounds for a similar purpose.)

5. Common Faults

(See *also* **Useful terms**, *p.* 22)

In a language which is constantly changing there is always some conflict between current usage and established practice. Similarly, there are differences between what is permissible in popular speech and what is expected in formal writing.

For a few of the constructions considered below there can be no hard-and-fast rules. (Such entries are marked with a *.)

1. Agreement

A singular subject must have a singular verb-form, a plural subject a plural verb-form. Be sure to ask yourself whether the subject is singular or plural.

e.g. *One* of the men *was* guilty.
A *range* of goods *was* available.
All along the coast *lie traces* of oil slick.

(a) Indefinite pronouns – i.e. 'anyone', 'someone', 'no one', 'none', '(n)either' (when used without '(n)or'), 'everyone', 'each' – are singular and should take a singular verb and be followed by 'he', 'him', 'his', and *not* 'they', 'them', 'their(s)': *

e.g. No one knows *his* own future.
Anyone can do it if *he* tries *his* best.
Each stood with *his* right hand behind *his* back.

(b) (N)either... (n)or. If *both* the subjects are singular, the verb is also:

e.g. Neither the man nor the dog *was* in sight.

If one or both of the subjects are plural, the verb is plural:

e.g. Neither John nor his friends *are* coming.

(c) this kind, this sort (or **these kinds, these sorts**), but not 'these kind', 'these sort'. *

(d) Collective nouns (which are groups of persons or things) take a singular verb when considered as a complete unit:

e.g. The class *is* too large.

But a plural verb when considered as a number of separate persons or things:

e.g. the class *were* quarrelling.

(e) The verb-form in an adjective clause must agree with the right noun (or pronoun) in the clause before it:

e.g. He is one of the most famous writers who *have* ever lived. ('Who' relates back to 'writers'; hence the plural 'have'.)

2 Case

(a) I, he, she, we, they, and **who** are the subject.
e.g. The man who will be king …

WRONG: John and me are brothers.
RIGHT: John and *I* are brothers.
WRONG: This is the man whom we all knew was guilty.
RIGHT: This is the man *who* (we all knew) was guilty.
(The brackets show that 'who' is the subject of 'was')
or: This is the man *whom* we all *knew to be* guilty.

(b) Me, him, her, us, them and **whom** are the object.

e.g. The man *whom* we met … (i.e. we met *him*.)

('Whom' seems to be dying out of the language, but should be kept after prepositions:
e.g. To whom shall I send it?
… for whom the bell tolls.
but not when *who* is the subject of a noun clause:
e.g. There was some doubt about who did it.)

WRONG: Thank you for inviting Joan and I to dinner.
RIGHT: Thank you for inviting Joan and *me* to dinner.
The object case is used after all prepositions:
WRONG: He gave it to John and I.
RIGHT: He gave it to John and *me*.
WRONG: between you and I; for you and he.
RIGHT: between you and *me*; for you and *him*.

3 The confusing of pronouns, especially 'one', 'you', 'it', 'he' and 'they'

(a) If you start using the word 'one' you must continue with it, though it can soon result in pomposity.

WRONG: One can easily spot your mistakes if you check carefully.
RIGHT: One can easily spot one's mistakes if one checks carefully.
(Or, better still, use 'you' and 'your'.)

(b) Make sure, when using pronouns like 'he' , 'she', 'it' and 'they', that it is absolutely clear to whom or to what they refer.

WRONG: If the baby does not like fresh milk, boil it.
RIGHT: Boil the milk, if the baby does not like it fresh.
WRONG: As the bomb fell into the car, it stopped dead.
RIGHT: The car stopped dead as the bomb fell into it.

(c) Do not confuse singular and plural.

WRONG: The marigold is a fairly hardy plant; they grow in most soils.

RIGHT: Marigolds are fairly hardy plants; they grow in most soils.

or: The marigold is a fairly hardy plant; it grows in most soils.

4 The comparative and the superlative

The **comparative** applies to two:
e.g. He is the better cricketer of the two.
The **superlative** applies to three or more:
e.g. He is the best swimmer in the county.

WRONG: John is the tallest of the two brothers.
RIGHT: John is the *taller* of the two brothers.

5 The participal phrase

This is introduced by a verb-form ending in '-ing' or '-ed' and describes the noun (or pronoun) nearest to it, but outside the phrase itself. Such phrases are often wrongly related, or unattached.

WRONG: Sitting on the veranda, the sun rose on our left. (This means that the sun was sitting on the veranda.)

RIGHT: Sitting on the veranda, *we* saw the sun rise on our left.

WRONG: Coming downstairs, the hall door opened. (This means that the hall door was coming downstairs.)

RIGHT: As he was coming downstairs, the hall door opened.

6 The gerund (or verbal noun)

This ends in '-ing' but acts as a *noun*; when qualified, it must, therefore, be preceded by an adjective (e.g. his, her, its, my, our, your, their):

WRONG: I don't like you leaving early.

RIGHT: I don't like your leaving early. (It is the 'leaving' I don't like.)

WRONG: I must escape without him knowing.

RIGHT: I must escape without *his* knowing.

7 The subjunctive

This is rarely used now, but watch out for:

(a) Pure supposition: e.g. If I *were* King …

(b) After verbs of wishing: e.g. I wish she *were* here.

(Also in 'Britannia *rule* the waves' and 'Long *live* the Queen'.)

8 The position of common adverbs (e.g. only, just, almost, even, mainly, also)

These should be placed immediately before the word they modify. Try inserting the word 'only' in every possible position in this sentence:
The bishop gave the baboon a bun.
(Consider the different meanings.)

Care must also be taken with the placing of 'both', '(n)either … (n)or' and 'not only … but also'.

WRONG: He not only plays tennis but also cricket.

RIGHT: He plays not only tennis but also cricket.
(The two parts must be correctly balanced.)

9 The correct preposition

(a) different *from* (or to, not 'than')

(b) to centre *on*, *in* or *upon* (not '(a)round')

(c) to prefer this *to* that (not 'than')

(d) anxious *about* (not 'of')

(e) bored *with* or *by* (not 'of')

(f) superior *to* (not 'than')

10 Words commonly confused

(a) *Lie* and *lay*. 'To lie' means to put yourself in a flat position; 'to lay' means to place something else (e.g. a plate) flat down.

To lie	*Present tenses*	I lie or am lying
	Past tenses	I *lay* or was lying
		I have *lain*
To lay	*Present tenses*	I lay it or am laying it down
	Past tenses	I *laid* it or was laying it down
		I have *laid* it down

(b) Shall and **will**

I/we *shall*, you/he/they *will* are the simple future tense.

I/we *will*, you/he/they *shall* express a strong wish or determination: e.g. They *shall* not pass. I *will* not give in.
(A person intent on suicide might say: "I *will* drown and nobody *shall* save me.")

(c) May, might, can

'Can' means 'to be able to'.

'May' is the present tense; 'might' is the past tense. (Both mean 'to be permitted'.)

'May' also expresses a distinct possibility: 'might' expresses the idea that it is just possible but unlikely.

(d) Each other and **one another; between** and **among**

'Each other' and 'between' refer to two people or things; 'one another' and 'among' refer to more than two:*

e.g. the duel they hurt *each other*.
The boys in the class were fighting *one another*.

(e) Due to and **owing to**

Use 'owing to' when you mean 'because of' and almost always at the beginning of a sentence. Use 'due to' (meaning 'caused by') as an adjective after the verb 'to be'. *

WRONG: Due to illness, he missed the game.
RIGHT: Owing to illness, he missed the game.
or: His absence was *due* to illness.

(Many people feel that this distiction can no longer be drawn.)

(f) Like and **as**

'Like' is a preposition (or an adjective) but not a conjunction. It should not be followed by a finite verb. Use 'as' if you mean 'in the same way *that*': *

WRONG: He talks like I do.
RIGHT: He talks *as* I do.

(g) Past and **passed**

Use 'passed' for the verb (and its past participle); 'past' for all other uses:
e.g. He passed me the ball. He has passed.
in the past (noun); he went past (adverb); in past ages (adjective); he ran past me (preposition).

(h) Of, off, have

WRONG: I must of made a mistake.
RIGHT: I must *have* made a mistake.
('Of' is not a verb.)

'Of' means belonging to or relating to. 'Off' means away from or down from a place:
e.g. He fell off the cliff.

(i) Stood, standing; sat, sitting

WRONG: I was stood; I was sat
(unless you really mean that someone else picked you up and put you in a standing or sitting position)
RIGHT: I *was standing* or I *stood*; I *was sitting* or I *sat*.

(j) All right/alright

Some consider 'alright' to be all wrong: others think that it offers a useful distinction (meaning fairly well or yes) from 'all right' (meaning all are correct). Use 'all right' for examination purposes.*

(k) Should and would

The main uses are:

(i) 'Should' or 'would' is used (depending on the person) as part of another verb expressing the future in the past:*
e.g. I/we *should* be glad …
you/he/she/they *would* be glad …

(ii) 'Should', used with all persons, also means 'ought to':
e.g. I/you/they *should* be playing in the team.

(iii) 'Should', also with all persons, is used for 'if' clauses:
e.g. If you should see him, give him my regards.

(iv) 'Would', with all persons, also expresses the idea of willingness:
e.g. I *would* play if I could.

(v) 'Would', with all persons, can also mean 'used to':
e.g. As a child he *would* play for hours.

11 Mixed constructions

(a) Faulty comparisons

WRONG: as good if not better than …
RIGHT: as good as if not better than …
or: at least as good as …

(b) Double negatives:

WRONG: I don't want nothing
RIGHT: I don't want anything.
or: I want nothing.
WRONG: He couldn't hardly believe it.
RIGHT: He could hardly believe it.

(c) Hardly/scarcely, when they mean 'no sooner … than', are followed by 'when' (or 'before'), not 'than':
e.g. He had hardly/scarcely written a page when/before the bell rang.

(d) Mixed tenses

WRONG: I should be glad if you will . . .
RIGHT: I should be glad if you would . . .
or: I shall be glad if you will . . .
WRONG: I have and always will be a football fan.
RIGHT: I have been, and always will be, a football fan.
WRONG: I didn't ought to have done it.
RIGHT: I ought not to have done it.
WRONG: I didn't use to ...
RIGHT: I used not to ...

(e) Order of adjectives

WRONG: the three first chapters (there is only one *first* chapter)
RIGHT: the first three chapters (meaning chapters one, two and three)

(f) Try to/try and ...

Normally use try *to*, except when you mean two separate actions:
e.g. try to aim high or you may try and fail.

(g) Between is followed by 'and' (not 'or'):
e.g. He had a choice between cricket *and* tennis.

(h) Comprise (meaning 'consist of', 'be composed of') does not need 'of':
e.g. The kit comprised (or was composed of) four items.

(i) And who/and which occurs only if who/which has already been used in the sentence.

(j) Don't repeat a preposition

WRONG: These are the subjects to which he must pay attention to.

(k) Them/those

WRONG: Give me them slippers.
RIGHT: Give me those slippers.

12 Misused words

(a) Literally means exactly to the letter, in actual fact.

WRONG: He literally flew down the street. (He didn't sprout wings.)

(b) Unique means the only one of its kind – like the phoenix. Strictly, things can't be quite unique or very unique. (Likewise with 'invaluable' (meaning priceless).)

(c) etc. This is an abbreviation of *et cetera*, meaning 'and the rest'. It should not be used lazily; specify what you have in mind. Don't write 'and etc.' 'ect.' or 'e.t.c.'

13 Redundancy (using more words than are necessary)

WRONG: He is equally as clever as his brother.
RIGHT: He is as clever as his brother.
WRONG: He fell off of his horse.
RIGHT: He fell off his horse.
WRONG: The reason why is because …
RIGHT: The reason is that …
or: This is because …
WRONG: Long ago since …
RIGHT: Long since …
WRONG: You're nearer my age than what she is.
RIGHT: You're nearer my age than she is.

'Assemble', 'co-operate', 'combine', 'mix' and 'mingle' do not normally require the word 'together'.
'Meet' is to be preferred to 'meet up with' and 'miss' to 'miss out on'.
Use 'just' or 'exactly', but not both.
'But' does not need 'however', 'yet' or 'nevertheless'.
'Return' does not need 'back'.
'As to' is often used unnecessarily, especially before 'whether'.
Avoid 'seeing as' – use 'as' or 'since'.

14 Mixed metaphors

These occur when you are not thinking and particularly when you are using overworked metaphors.
e.g. I smell a rat but I'll nip it in the bud.

15 Ambiguity (confusion of meaning)

This is often caused by:

(a) unclear pronouns:
e.g. She likes me more than you.
This could mean
either: She likes me more than she likes you.
or: She likes me more than you do.

Generally, ask yourself if it is clear to whom or what the pronoun refers, especially when you are using 'it' or 'they', and 'as' or 'than'.

(b) wrong punctuation or word order:
e.g. The door opened and a young woman carrying a baby and her husband entered.
(See also sub-sections 3 and 8 above.)

16 Words overworked or loosely used

(a) 'Nice', 'good', 'bad', 'lovely', 'fine', 'real', 'get'

Over-using any word can cause monotony and blunt meaning, but the above are usually too vague or loosely colloquial for accurate writing, though they can sometimes be used with force.

'Get', though often too colloquial, may at times be the most natural expression. (e.g. He got off the bus.)

Other popular words which are loosely used are:
fantastic, fabulous, tremendous, terrific, great, incredible, diabolical, ghastly, definitely
In general, look for a more precise word.

(b) In formal writing avoid colloquialisms and slang (i.e. expressions from common speech like 'lots of', 'bloke', 'a bit of alright', 'chickened out'). Avoid, too, loose, vague expressions like 'a good thing'.

(c) Clichés (i.e. very common over-used expressions) like 'this day and age', 'no way', 'the thin end of the wedge', 'stand up and be counted', and 'right across the board' should be avoided 'like the plague'!

(d) 'Then', 'so' and 'suddenly'. Often casually used or over-used by young writers, these words can cause disjointedness and dullness. Give more thought to varied, logical and effective sentence construction.